TO:

. . . .

FROM:

. . . .

DATE:

. . . .

YOU are EXTRAORDINARY

Craig and Samantha Johnson
Illustrated by Sally Garland

Tommy NELSON

An Imprint of Thomas Nelson

This book is for all the children who have ever felt less than the amazing, incredible, spectacular person God created you to be. You are perfect just the way you are! Whether you are typical, are medically fragile, or have special needs, we hope this book reminds you every day that

YOU ARE EXTRAORDINARY!

Published in Nashville, Tennessee, by Tommy Nelson. Tommy Nelson is an imprint of Thomas Nelson. Thomas Nelson is a registered trademark of HarperCollins Christian Publishing, Inc.

Written by Jean Fischer.

Illustrated by Sally Garland.

Tommy Nelson titles may be purchased in bulk for educational, business, fund-raising, or sales promotional use. For information, please email SpecialMarkets@ThomasNelson.com.

Scripture quotations are taken from the International Children's Bible®. Copyright © 1986, 1988, 1999, 2015 by Thomas Nelson. Used by permission. All rights reserved.

Library of Congress Cataloging-in-Publication Data

Names: Johnson, Craig E. (Craig Edward), 1952- author. | Garland, Sally Anne, illustrator.

Title: You are extraordinary / Craig and Samantha Johnson ; illustrated by Sally Garland.

Description: Nashville : Thomas Nelson, 2019. |

Identifiers: LCCN 2018051188 (print) | LCCN 2019000343 (ebook) | ISBN 9781400209163 (e-book) | ISBN 9781400209132 (hardcover)

Subjects: LCSH: Identity (Psychology)--Religious aspects--Christianity--Juvenile literature. | Identity (Psychology) in children--Juvenile literature.

Classification: LCC BT705 (ebook) | LCC BT705 .J64 2019 (print) | DDC 242/.62--dc23

LC record available at https://lccn.loc.gov/2018051188

ISBN-13: 978-1-4002-0913-2

Printed in China

19 20 21 22 23 DSC 6 5 4 3 2 1

Mfr: DSC / Shenzhen, China / May 2019 / PO #9537423

Foreword

Our words have creative power. Whenever we speak something, either good or bad, we give life to what we are saying. I have watched Craig and Samantha speak victory over their children, telling them, "I'm proud of you. I love you. You are amazing. You are talented. You are beautiful. You will do great things in life." As parents, when we speak words like these over our kids, we are blessing our children's futures.

—Joel Osteen

Letter to Parents

All parents have a moment when they sit face-to-face with their children to have an important conversation. The conversations may look a little different, but they have the same goal: to let kids know that they are exceptional, unique, and wonderful just as they are.

For the little girl who gets picked on based on the color of her skin

For the young boy struggling with autism

For the kid who is bullied because he's different

For the child in a wheelchair

For the little one who is adopted

For the smart girl who's always being made fun of

For the brave little fighter battling illness

You Are Extraordinary is for all children who need a moment of reassurance that God has a plan for their lives, that they are so loved, and—what might be the most important message—that the world is a better place when we treat all people like they are extraordinary. We hope this book will be a catalyst to point your children to their destinies and give them the encouragement they need to succeed.

—Craig and Samantha

Your life is so precious. You're God's gift from above.

Each thing about you is something I love.

God made you just right—but not ordinary.

He made you perfectly

Extra Ordinary!

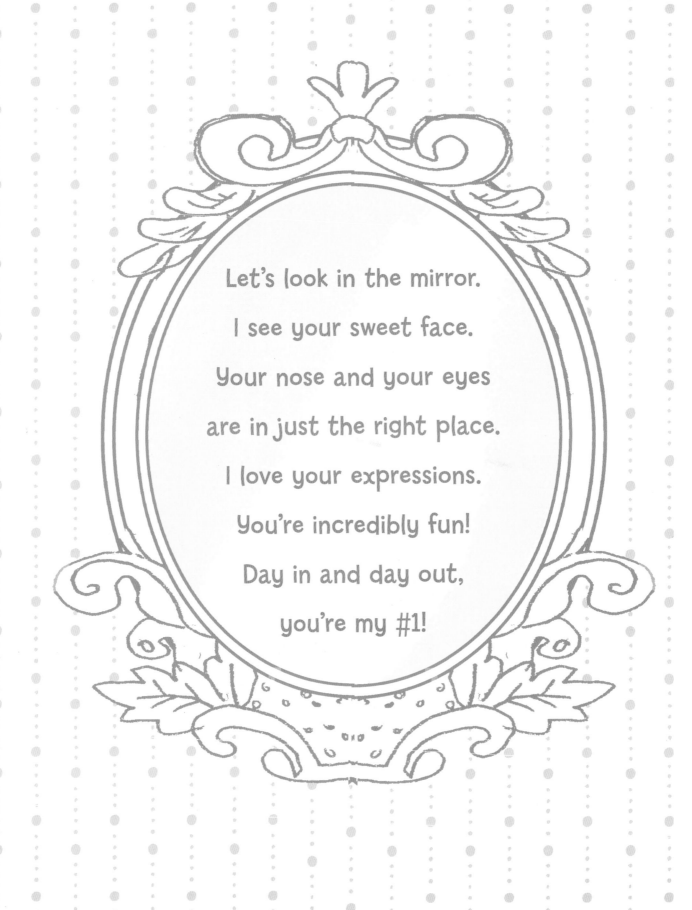

Let's look in the mirror.

I see your sweet face.

Your nose and your eyes

are in just the right place.

I love your expressions.

You're incredibly fun!

Day in and day out,

you're my #1!

All families are special. No two are the same.

Each has its own people. Each has its own name.

Our family has *you*, and that **MAKES** it the **BEST**,

Delightfully different

and unlike

the **REST**.

I know who you are,   and I see what you do.

I love this **amazing,** **incredible YOU!**

Whenever you're challenged by things that go wrong,

I like how you face it! You stay brave and strong.

You've learned how to do things with your **SPECIAL STYLE**.

When it's hard or it hurts, you still

MANAGE TO SMILE.

On days when you're sick or you must stay in bed
Or you're worried about what the doctor has said,

God's **LOVE** gets you through it. You know that He's close.

You can feel His big love when you need it *the*

MOST.

Some days you'll feel happy.

Some days you'll feel sad.

And sometimes your feelings won't *feel* good or bad.

Whatever you're feeling, this one thing is true—

I always will love my **EXCEPTIONAL YOU!**

I know that you learn in
your own unique way.

Some learning takes time,
and some takes just a day.

But when all the hard work
of learning is through,

I'm **HAPPY** and **PROUD**
that you've learned something new.

Some days you don't care for big groups that are loud.
You need your own space far away from the crowd.
But **OH**, the **AMAZING** and **SMART** things you do

When you're all by yourself

and just being you.

And when you feel lonely and don't know what to do,

Remember that others feel loneliness too.

So if you feel brave

and have time

you can spend,

Consider that

SOMEONE

NEEDS

YOU

as a friend.

A friend can be short, or a friend can be tall.

And how a friend looks doesn't matter at all!

But whoever you meet, remember what's right—

WE ALL DESERVE LOVE, so we're all just alike.

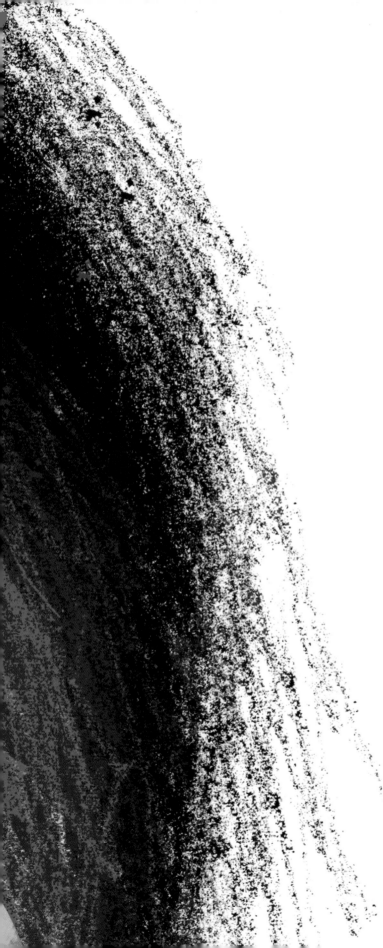

God gave you a purpose.

With His love and grace,

You'll help make this world

A MUCH

BETTER PLACE.

He gave you ideas

and talents to use

So you can succeed

AT WHATEVER

YOU CHOOSE.

God knows who you are, and He sees what you do.

He made this amazing, incredible **YOU**!

He made you just right. You're a bright shining star,

And I'll love you forever just as you are.

YOU ARE EXTRAORDINARY!

Dear God, I praise You because You made me in an amazing and wonderful way.

Amen.

PSALM 139:14 ICB